With Open Eyes

With Open Eyes

RICK ROBINSON

authorHOUSE®

AuthorHouse™ UK Ltd.
500 Avebury Boulevard
Central Milton Keynes, MK9 2BE
www.authorhouse.co.uk
Phone: 08001974150

First published by AuthorHouse   5/12/2010

ISBN: 978-1-4490-9655-7 (sc)

This book is printed on acid-free paper.

Fill the world
with gasps
Not sighs
As you look at it
With open eyes

Introduction

This is not a single story although you will find some tales among its pages. It started off as observations just scribbled down after I had returned from my walks out in the countryside. It was for my own benefit really, just so I would be able, in later years to look back on my jottings and remember. Then it started to take hold, I began to write about everything because everything seemed to have a story to tell. I think it was maybe my questioning nature. You see I can't help but wonder why is that song thrush singing atop that holly bush, or what that aged yew tree may have seen through its long life? Then there are just happenings, which perhaps mean nothing until you stop and think about them. A frosty January morning or a heat filled August day, this is what this little book is all about. Some of the essays in this book happened, some didn't, some of them might have done, but we will never know. Others well they are a mixture of both fact and little bit of artistic license, which I believe authors are allowed to use.

I will make no apologies if you don't like what you are about to read, but I really hope you do. And I would like to think I have managed to put into words some of the enjoyment being outdoors has given me. Then perhaps when you put this book down you might be tempted to step outside and see what's really out there. You might just get a surprise.

Contents

1. A Brief Moment 1
2. The Field 3
3. Curiosity 5
4. Sky 9
5. All Hallows Eve 10
6. Sounds 13
7. Great Journey 15
8. Not Just Blue 17
9. Lesser Celandine 19
10. Alone 20
11. A Perfect River 25
12. Lucy 27
13. September 30
14. Two Foxes 32
15. White and Green 35
16. They Missed Out 37
17. Herald of Summer 39
18. A Long Hot Summer 41
19. Hero 43
20. Trees 46
21. The Halcyon Bird 47
22. Signs Of Spring 51
23. Rain Watching 53
24. Look Next Time 55
25. A Different Kind Of Jewel 56
26. Not What I Expected 60
27. The Watcher 62
28. The Loneliest Conker Tree in the Whole World 65
29. Dusk 67

A Brief Moment

As you lay in your bed
awaiting your time to rise.
Think of what you may be missing,
It could well be a greater prize

Who would have believed a single drop of water could have such a dramatic effect? That it would leave a memory that would remain long after that single drop had journeyed countless miles through streams and rivers and out into the sea. It is still etched into my memory and I can pull it out at will, I can put myself back into that very same place I saw it. Just by closing my eyes and remembering. I can feel the chill on my cheeks, see my breath rise into the cold, early morning air and watch it until it disappears into the dark bare branches above my head. Beneath my boots there is the crunching of heavily frosted grass and as I disturb the leaf litter a damp musty smell arrives at my nostrils.

There are snowdrops, and over there in the bottom most branches of an old Yew tree, a flock of small birds are singing. Then as I draw my head towards them they flit between the branches and out of sight with an almost gay abandon. The sun is beginning to break through the milky haze and force its way into this winter wonderland. Slowly at first, little fingers of light probing their way into the still sleeping woodland. The light growing brighter by the second. Opening new vistas and gnawing away at the freezing nights build up of hoar frost. As the sun rises higher into the early morning sky the pace quickens. Its warmth becoming more evident, the grass is less rigid and the ground begins to soften. As ice turned to water I first noticed it, a bright jewel fit to grace any ring. The sun having made the beautiful crystal globe, now glinted off it, and sparkled through it. This delicate gem demanded my attention I knelt down next to it, very carefully not wanting to be responsible for the destruction of such a fragile beauty. Ignoring the damp penetrating through my trousers and onto my knees. I leant forward now lying right next to it, almost touching it. Up close it took on a different life, both elegant and fragile, it mirrored its surroundings. Deep within the globe I could see, the bright green of the grass and the glow of the ever-lightening sky. I watched it grow as the warming air nibbled away at the frost and added to the liquid diamond that now hung precariously from the tip of a blade of grass. An upside down world of trees and sky showed itself to me through that little drop of water. Slowly growing until too heavy for that single blade, the inevitable came to pass. Almost in slow motion the grass gave up its prize. It fell and smashed onto the earth below, gone forever. A once seen jewel never to be repeated unless that is until I care to remember.

The Field

What is now?
has not always been

There used to be a field. A beautiful, lush emerald green, grass field. I can't remember it ever being grazed by sheep or cattle, but I suppose it must have been at some time as there was a large stone drinking trough in it. It was down in the bottom corner, beneath an imposing old Oak tree, that seemed to me, to be standing guard over this green oasis. During the spring and early summer the field went through a huge transition in what seemed a matter of just a few days. My walk to school was no longer a chore and I began to view the changes with ever widening eyes.

As the days lengthened and got warmer so the grass grew taller, but it wasn't just green that greeted me each morning. Slowly at first, a change began to take place. It started with a few yellow buttercups appearing and then the odd purple and blue of thistle and forget-me-not, with pink cranesbills not far behind. More flowers showing each day, the yellows of trefoil and dandelion, to be quickly joined by a few pink field orchids, bright red campion and still more yellow as cowslips joined the show.

These in turn looked up to ox-eye daisies and brilliant scarlet poppies. The grass too had begun to change as silver seed heads hung down heavily and gently nodded and swayed in the light breeze.

All of a sudden as if magically the field had changed, almost as though an artist had accidentally spilt his paints over a huge green canvas, but unlike a painting the scene was ever changing.

The grass growing taller and the flowers fighting to keep their place in the sun. Each day new ones appearing and others disappearing as there job was done. As the sun grew stronger with each passing day the canvas became framed by the white flowers of elder and hawthorn which had now filled the hedgerows surrounding the field. The heady scent having an almost hypnotic effect and the mass display of flowers promising a bumper crop of berries come the autumn.

As the field bloomed in a myriad of colours, insect life now became abundant and bees could be seen dancing from one flower to the next. Butterflies came to join the vibrant scene chasing one another over a multi-coloured playground. Red admirals, peacocks, ringlets and a never-ending parade of whites added their elegance and grace, as the picture became alive with movement. The hedgerows filled with the noise of newly hatched chicks of blackbird, dunnock and wren. The eager chicks demanding yet another meal from their overworked parents. The clear blue skies were filled with swallows feeding up on the abundant insect life as they waited their turn to raise a family.

I can see the whole picture now as I write this down; it's all there right down to the tiny pink orchid. It's such a shame that the field isn't. It has been gone quite a few years now taken away by mans ever increasing march into the countryside. The only greens, blues and yellows remaining now are brightly shining cars and garishly painted front doors. The only pinks on show are the uniformly laid out straight lines of geraniums and roses. Gone is the long grass to be replaced by gravel drives and neatly manicured lawns with not even a daisy in sight. All together in a frame of black tarmac and grey concrete.

There used to be a field....

Curiosity

Where once was green now is grey
Where once was soft now is hard
Where once was life now is death

What was this strange and wonderful sight that greeted the young badger cub? For what seemed an age, but had in fact only been four short weeks his perception of life had been so different. Those first few weeks of his life, his world had been one of darkness and warmth. Everything he knew and experienced had come by way of scent and sound. The smells and noises created by his extended family were all he knew and understood. Occasionally an adult would return from wherever they went, and with it would come something new. A strange never before experienced scent. Sometimes sweet, sometimes damp and once a horrible sharp acrid smell that made the youngster retreat back to the security of his mother. The cub was learning the skills to survive in a world of what would be a life spent in the dark of the night. He and countless young cubs before him had been taught the first lessons of life deep underground on this same wooded hillside. For nearly 200 years the set had flourished and still now each night the woodland floor became a playground and larder for badgers. Yes there had been a new road built nearby but the badgers soon began to understand the hard learnt lessons and dangers of motor cars, but this young cub was not yet ready for that. He needed teaching about roots, plants and fungi and slowly he was learning, from his ever-attentive mother.

That time for learning would have to wait for now and as he stood at the entrance to the set; he began to recognize some of those scents that had invaded his early life. This was where the adults went.

Although the sun was still high in the pale blue spring sky, the young cub had crept away from his still sleeping family. Leaving behind the warmth of his brothers and sisters and security of his mother's warm fur. Never before had he even left the nest chamber, but curiosity had first woken and then nudged the cub along the long dark tunnels. Where did the adults go? Where did the fresh bedding come from? What were those strange scents? What else was there? Questions the young cub needed an answer to.

At first he had crept slowly staying tight to the tunnel walls, their touch giving a familiar security as he inched his way forward, further away from all he had known and the protection of his sleeping family. Closer towards the smell of the clean air that had filtered down and now lured him ever upward. Up towards something, he knew not what but the urge was growing stronger and could not be quelled. His pace quickened no longer pressing himself against the walls of the tunnel, but scampering upward. Until turning a sharp bend he slowed as he became aware of a soft light, faint at first but getting brighter with every paw he placed in front of another. Up towards a light he had never known existed until now. He began sniffing at the clean smelling air, laden heavy with so many scents and there was one he recognized. The same fragrance that he had smelt on his mother's coat, although he did not yet have a picture to match the perfume of the bluebell. As he scrambled his way those last few feet to the mouth of the set, his squinting eyes were, presented with the young cubs first ever Spring day. In fact, his first ever day out in the light. He was presented with colours he had never seen, sounds he had never heard and the smells, what a fantastic array of fragrances. The cub's senses were being bombarded by the information he was trying to take in. It was all too much and he recoiled into the reassuring half light of the set entrance. Curiosity and excitement had been replaced by fear, fear of the unknown. There he stood with only his inquisitive nostrils visible trying to make sense of what was out there. He thought briefly of his snuffling and snoring siblings back down in the dark, but soon forgot as he noticed for the first time his own black and white coat. He looked upon his little claws protruding from his paws. Yes he had known they were there but he had never seen them before, he had never really seen anything before. He looked up and there in front of him was a whole new world, until now unknown to him. Greens, browns and blues, movement and light what a place this was. The young cub stared in awe at the scene that greeted him. The trees that towered above him their topmost branches out of sight seeming to disappear into the sky. All around was bird song that sounded so enchanting to one who had only ever heard grunts and growls, and the child like squeals of his brothers and sisters as they squabbled over their mother's milk. A vast arena beckoned him to leave the confines of his known world and come and explore. Slowly at first, curiosity began to replace his fear and he took his first few steps into this strange and wonderful world. Each paw placed down on unfamiliar ground as the earthen floor was replaced by last year's fallen leaves. Then a soft green that demanded the young badger cub to roll and gambol through it. Lost in play the badger ran, chasing the breeze that tugged at his fur, until at the bottom of the slope he stopped abruptly. He raised his nose to the air, a scent he was familiar with. He had lain among its fronds in the nest chamber. It was the fern his parents had collected and changed so diligently these past weeks. He followed the scent perhaps in expectation of company. He pushed his way through the fresh growth of some nettles, startling a couple of squabbling blackbirds who were even more surprised than the young badger. They rose quickly into the air quickly forgetting their differences as they disappeared in opposite directions. Driven on by an urge to explore the cub strayed further and further from the set. He stopped to watch a young rabbit nibbling away at some fresh green shoots and once again he longed for some company. The rabbit though was not interested and as soon as it became aware of the badger, it skipped quickly out of the dappled shade with just a couple of bounds.

Left alone in the clearing the cub sat and watched as strange insects scurried away from him and buzzed around his ears. As the still warm sun penetrated through the early spring growth of the trees warmth swept over him and an urge to sleep consumed him. Surrounded by birdsong, such beautiful notes that he seemed to remember from a dream as he had nestled into his mother's fur. The warm air and soothing song, the sweet smell of bluebells and gentle buzzing of the bees. They all combined in an almost hypnotic effect and as he lay on the soft grass his eyes began to close and sleep took over.

Who knows how long he slept, but he woke with a start, he was cold and alone. Gone was the warm sun the light was fading, not yet dark but day time was giving way to night. Gone too was the bird song in fact it was quiet apart from the distant harsh calls of rooks returning to roost after a day feeding out in the fields. There was also a low growling noise, just the other side of the hedge and it was getting louder. Could it be another badger come to scold him and take him home? He hoped so, the rooks seemed to be mocking him now as they took to their lofty perches their cawing louder and threatening. He needed to get away; he needed to find his mother. He pushed his way through the prickly hedge the thorns pressing against him as he squeezed through the tightest of gaps. Then quicker, expectantly up the steep bank the other side and all the time the distant growling getting louder, getting closer. Then up out of the dyke bottom.

What was that strange feeling underfoot it was hard and uncomfortable, almost painful. There was that strange acrid smell he remembered from the set. There was something else, was that the same rabbit he had seen earlier in the day? Why didn't it move? It was just lying there still and lifeless.

The growling was getting louder.

Sky

Blue sky above
but only for a short while

Have you ever looked at the sky? I mean really looked, not just a cursory glance to see if it's going to rain or whether to pack your coat into the car. I mean a long look, a searching look, so that you notice the different colours and shades. Not just the bright blue of a beautiful summer's day or the dark grey of the storm clouds but the bits in between. That inky blue time just before daylight bids us goodbye, or that cold winters sky full of calling geese. Then there is the slow waking of a spring morning's sky that fills us with expectancy. Of course we also have that brilliant red sunset that shepherds hold in such high esteem and that star filled sky of a frosty winters evening.

It's not just about white fluffy clouds or the bright orange sun disappearing over a turquoise sea, but all that little bits in between.

All Hallows Eve

The green garb of the hunter
the black mask of the highwayman
finished with a crimson hood
"Hail the wood sprite"

October 31st.

All hallows eve. Half past six and it was already getting dark the clocks only went back last night and already I'm wondering how I will get through the long dark nights ahead. Evenings spent stuck in the house in front of the fire, just longing for spring. I will have to find a way to fill my evenings, without an after tea excursion down by the river, across the fields or through the woods. Well tonight I won't have that problem, because a continual stream of goblins, ghosts and ghouls keep pulling me away from my reading to eagerly demand a treat from me. Or else I shall suffer the non-too pleasant consequences of a trick.

I was reading an old book on the folklore of birds and as I flicked through it I came across a few pages on the green woodpecker. This got me to thinking, only two evenings ago at about this very same time I had been out walking through the woods that fringed the river, not a mile from my home. The loud laughter like cry of a green woodpecker had alerted me to its presence, and as I looked up into the still bright sky the characteristic up and down flight confirmed what my ears had told me. I watched as it perched itself halfway up the trunk of a huge poplar tree. Well perhaps perched is the wrong word as there was nothing to perch on just a straight trunk, but this offered no obstacle to the woodpecker as he worked his way up and around the trunk. Stopping every so often to feed and look around.

Whereas then I had stood watched him for 15 minutes, I was now staring at the black and white text in front of me. Having to remember the beautiful slim green body and the golden rump, the bright red cap and black robbers mask. That was two days ago now, the clocks going back had changed things, for me anyway.

"Knock, knock."

A couple of the undead demanding sweets, and as I watched them disappear into the night a cold wind blew into my doorway and signalled my retreat indoors. As I left behind the cold night air for the refuge of my centrally heated home, I quickly closed the door after me and turned up the thermostat on the heating.

I thought of the woodpecker, secure and warm in its moss lined roosting hole. The feathers all fluffed up for extra insulation, not even noticing as the temperature fell a few more degrees and the cold north wind began to blow a little stronger. The roosting hole had been excavated with just such a night in mind. Although it was still spring when work had begun, the entrance hole was deliberately faced on the south side of the tree. The biting cold of a winter's northerly gale would not find its way into this haven from the weather.

Now while my evening was accompanied by the constant drone of the television set in the front room and the intermittent gurgle of the dishwasher. The woodpecker could hear things that were just as familiar to it. The sound of the wind in the trees. The topmost branches constantly knocking together as they swayed to and fro with the wind. There was the loud screech of a tawny owl and the snapping of twigs below, as the badgers bundled their way through the undergrowth looking for a tasty morsel. Away from the woods towards the town two dog foxes were barking out their territory, daytime had given way to night.

"Knock knock".

On my way back from another ghostly experience at the front door I flicked on the kettle and thought maybe a couple of chocolate biscuits. No thoughts of food for the woodpecker he had spent the morning feeding up on insects, he had found in the meadow. Then in the afternoon winkling out grubs and insects from beneath the bark of rotting trees. Then late on just before the sun disappeared he had returned to one of his regular haunts, an ant's nest, in an old willow stump, and there he had eaten his fill. His long sticky tongue extracting the ants with a consummate ease.

There it was the click of the kettle; I would have to make that coffee now.

"Knock, knock".

I wondered what would greet me this time, a couple of witches and a very small vampire. Great costumes they had really made an effort and hanging off their lanterns each one had a little toy bat suspended by elastic.

"Well done lads chocolate all round".

The woodpecker too could also see bats. Every evening they left their roost under the old railway bridge to feed on the moths that seemed to thrive in the woods. Their swift zigzagging flight between the trees a spectacle for anyone or anything that was able to see it. The woodpecker was able to admire their flying skills without even leaving the warmth of his home, if it so wished.

As I walked through the dining room I noticed the newspaper spread out on the table. The headline read *"Interest rates to rise in USA" and* for some reason I read it. What was I doing? Do I care? Does it really matter to me what happens thousands of miles away the other side of the Atlantic Ocean? I must confess to being a bit unimpressed with global matters. Even what happens at the other end of town fails to get me too interested. Just like the woodpecker, I suppose if it doesn't really affect his food source or make him more vulnerable it didn't matter.

"Knock, knock".

Oh no not again I was fast running out of treats. A ghost and a zombie, albeit not a very impressive one. Mini bars each and one for me

"Good night kids".

Once again I closed the door behind me hoping that perhaps that was the last one for the night. Back to my book now and I headed into the conservatory carefully averting my eyes away from the newspaper. Then I settled down on the nice soft sofa we have in there, picked up my book and began to read, letting the warmth of the house take its effect on me. The big cushions seemed to offer a warm and comfortable haven from the cold outside. Perhaps winter evenings were not going to be so bad after all.

Out of the moss beneath the woodpecker crept an unsuspecting woodlouse. Only to be grabbed and gobbled up by the sharp bill of its host, who now put its head beneath its wing. And as the wind began to ease and the branches of the trees slowed to a gentle sway, the bird closed its eyes and dreamt of warm sunny days and huge anthills. I too drifted off to sleep and also began to dream of warm sunny days, watching woodpeckers. Although my dreams featured zombies and

Vampires, for some reason.

"Knock, knock, knock"

Sounds

Just listen
and you will hear

Just abandon the comfort of your favourite armchair and forgo the visual delights of daytime television. Leave behind the noise of your neighbour's lawn mower and the intruding ring of your doorbell and get out into the real world. I don't mean go for a ride in your car, stop off in a lay-by for a quick sandwich. Then rush home for no other reason than it's getting late or it's nearly tea time. Get out into the countryside, savour it, enjoy it. There is somewhere for all of us not too far away. Away from everything and everyone. Just keep walking until the sound of distant traffic has long ceased to be a distant hum. A knock at the door can't disturb you here. Oh yes, I nearly forgot that annoying little item that we all seem to depend on nowadays. The mobile phones, if you made the mistake of bringing it with you, turn it off. You don't want anything to disturb you. Once all the sounds of modern life have been left behind look around you for somewhere to settle down. Just over there in the lee of the hedge or perhaps beneath the dappled shade of an old tree. Maybe even in the middle of a field or you could always try my favourite, next to a river or a stream. It really doesn't matter. Now lie down, yes you can sit but I prefer to lie down. Move away the twigs and pebbles that are sticking in your back and making you uncomfortable, then close your eyes and listen. I don't mean think about work and listen or wonder how much your electric bill is going to be and listen. I mean just listen. There are no ticking clocks or background music from your children's bedroom. no crying babies or whirring of washing machines, but there are sounds. Sounds we have forgot sounds that perhaps we have never heard. The softness of the wind as it blows through the barley, the chirping of the grasshoppers. The song of the skylarks and what about butterfly's wings do they really make a sound when they touch.

I do hope so.

Great Journey

A great journey
deserves a great end

Over 6000 miles truly a great journey. A greater journey than most of us would ever contemplate even on an aeroplane. Even then it seems an awfully long way, but they had no choice. Leaving behind the clear blue sky's and sweltering heat of West Africa they set off heading north, just as they had always done. Through desert sandstorms and lightning filled clouds. On they flew the throng growing larger as they journeyed north. Like a relentless tide over hills and mountains, savannah and forests.

The sun reflecting off the azure blue waters of the Mediterranean, the first sign that the birds were drawing near. Was it an inbred fear of the distant coastline that made the birds falter a little. Or was it the sound of gunfire as gallic hungers took their turn at reducing the bird's numbers. A lot more effective than the talons of hungry hawks that had accompanied them from the journeys start. Their constant threat seeking out the weak and slow.

Getting closer now a distant coastline surrounded with low cloud and damp cool air. Where was the fanfare their journey deserved? They would have to wait as the land below had not yet woken from its winter slumber. Their reward would come in the next few weeks with a rise in the temperature allowing them to feed for perhaps 18 out of the 24 hours. That was a reward worth travelling for, for both themselves and their young.

Pushing themselves up over the clouds, one last push from those tiny wings. One last effort and then down into green rolling hills and quiet country lanes, lined with ancient trees and hedgerows. Down into a landscape of woods filled with primrose and bluebell, a world that held so much promise for its visitors.

Here for years the swallows had come to breed and raise their young in empty barns and sheds. As they came over the clouds the sun showed itself as if in greeting, lighting up the countryside below. Gliding now the effort gone from their wings, the air filled with chatter as the migration neared its end. Old friendships renewed as thoughts turned to last year's nests. Would they have survived the winter?

Would they be taken? The answer to both questions would soon be answered and is answered every May time in Britain, as the relentless invasion of our green and pleasant land continues.

Not Just Blue

Different shades
different hues
different days
different moods

Blue it seems such an ordinary and unemotional word, not really descriptive enough for what I want to convey, but yes it was blue. That special blue that you only get on very warm spring days. Not that soft pastel blue of the male common blue butterfly that can be seen feeding alongside country lanes throughout the summer. Nor was it the bright metallic blue that you see when you catch a glimpse of a kingfisher, it was neither or these. It was a soft but meaningful shade, announcing to the world that the cold days of winter could be confined to our memories for the next few months. A new warmth was spreading through the land, an unstoppable force was coming and nothing could halt its relentless march. The pale blue sky contrasted sharply with the fresh new growth of the trees. The sap had risen slowly at first and then burst forth with a flourish. In an explosion of vibrant bright greens, which now had begun to clothe the dark skeletal branches of the previous month? A loud hoarse call brought my attention down onto the woodland floor. There among the different shades of violets a Jay busied itself searching for the last of his acorn store from the previous autumn. The bright blue wing patches and pink body a strange choice of camouflage.

All around could be heard the excited calls of birds laying claim to new territories. The chiff chaff and the willow warblers announcing their presence to anything that was prepared to listen. Their songs reaching a crescendo, stopping and then almost instantly starting up again. The distant drumming of a woodpecker could be heard

through the trees, along with the constant chattering of a couple of magpies. In the branches above my head a little group of blue tits busied themselves, their blue caps and yellow breasts making them seem an almost tropical bird. They flitted from branch to looking for a meal. Then suddenly as if they had investigated every possible nook and cranny or just got bored of looking, they flew off across the river to an aged alder tree. The storms of the previous week had taken their toll on its precarious grip on the overhanging river bank, and it now bent over at an alarming angle. It would soon to become a casualty but for now its lower branches dipped into and disturbed the crystal clear waters. Beneath the branches a shoal of silver roach faced into the swift flow. The occasional fish rising to take an unsuspecting fly encouraged out by the unusually warm day. The roach then slowly sinking back down to take its place among its companions. At the edges of the river stood a large bank of water iris waiting their turn to flower, their huge buds promising a bumper display of yellow flowers in the coming weeks. Where the iris stems met the water a couple of mallard dabbled around . The male in all its grandeur, while the females single dark metallic blue wing feather a strange addition to its drab brown costume. Together they forced their way into the delicate mass of water forget-me-not. The sky blue flowers beginning a flowering season that would last all summer and not disappear completely until the first frosts. That was many months away and right now all around the countryside was full of the vigour of new life. Beneath the trees was a fresh bright green growth of a new growing season, nettles, comfrey and arum forcing their way upwards? Among the new growth its time in the sun nearly done, but still showing the cold cobalt blue were the last of the bluebells, that only a few weeks ago had carpeted the woodland floor and filled the air with a heady scent. The first Tufted Vetch flowers of the year had begun to show themselves, along with light blue Borage flowers now established along the grassy path that led to the old lock keepers cottage.

Yes, I was having a blue day but it was nothing to do with my mood. What a tremendous variety of blues I had seen in twenty minutes and I hadn't moved a foot. Next time someone tells you something is blue ask them what sort of blue they mean, kingfisher blue, forget-me-not blue, blue bell blue.

"IT'S NOT JUST BLUE".

Lesser Celandine

Gold is not always hidden

Lesser Celandine, well if that's the case I would really like to see a greater one. There at the bottom of the dyke, out of the cold wind and basking in the March sunshine. A carpet of brightly shining gold. Is there a more magnificent flower to bid us good day? Eight petals of highly polished gold that shout at you to come closer. From that tight bronze bud of yesterday is today's shining light. It had only needed a tiny bit of encouragement; just an hour in the sun was enough to change the landscape. Just an hour in the sun was enough to lighten my heart and make me realise what a wise decision it was, to have walked out of my front door on this cold and windy March day.

Alone

We recognise the cuckoos call,
the skylarks song one and all,
a calling owl brings us fear,
are we sure what it is we hear

Just the usual, a large flock of Canada geese, a few coots and then the odd group of ducks bobbing up and down on the still slightly choppy water. The storm of the previous couple of days not quite said its goodbyes just yet. I suppose I was hoping that the fierce winds might have blown a few birds off course and sent something out of the ordinary my way. Perhaps a tired finch or rare duck dropped down to the lakeside for a bit of refuge from the winds. Well, lake might be too grand a word for it; really it was more a disused gravel pit. It had been there perhaps one hundred and fifty years and owed its existence to the not to distant malting. They now, were also disused but the building of them all those years ago had demanded vast quantities of sand and gravel, and that was the beginning of this watery oasis on the edge of town. The now almost derelict malting stood as a ruined gateway into the once thriving market town, now a sad monument to its past prosperity. The malting decline had been watched by this body of water which had seemed to flourish as the years had been cruel to its red brick sentinel.

A huge body of deep water with a couple of tree clad islands, sitting centrally and lording over their surroundings. Trees and shrubs now crowded its once bare banks but gave way to the water at the steep declining edges. Wildlife had come to the trees and surrounding hedgerows and made this place a haven for birds among the intensely farmed fields surrounding it. The cormorant certainly wasn't a passing bird, he had always been a resident as long as I could remember, and there he sat high on his usual perch. Out on the island atop an old creaking willow he watched, safe in the knowledge nothing could bother him. Perhaps he was too full to fly after spending the morning gorging himself in the fish rich waters.

My attention turned to the rafts of ducks that had come into view from the back of one of the islands. I scanned them through my binoculars more in hope than expectation. Just the resident mallards and the odd tufted duck even a few Pochard had joined them for the winter. Yes they were beautiful, but today I just thought I may have seen something a little bit different. Close to the island there was a man made raft, where fly fisherman used to moor boats. A perfect spot to spend long lazy summer evenings, but that was a few years ago now when the water was a renowned trout fishery. I can remember as a young child watching, as green clad men wiled away their time flicking out an assortment of different coloured flies, in anticipation of landing one of the waters prized rainbow trout. These events were now confined to fisherman tales of summers past and the raft had long since become a roost for gulls. A safe platform away from predators and there they now sat perhaps a dozen of them. The white of the gulls a lot easier on the eye, after the grey sky, dark hedgerows and black forbidding water. Looking decidedly lethargic they sat around preening themselves or just sleeping. The small black dot behind their eyes identified them as black headed gulls, their dark head gone for the winter. As I checked through them with my binoculars, I became aware of a different bird among them right at the back almost hidden. Yes it was black and white maybe a tufted duck climbed up onto the raft. I waited for a better view and as a couple of gulls took to the air it revealed itself to me.

A slim white body black on top and white beneath, long pink legs, perching red eye and yes an unmistakable long orange bill. It was an oystercatcher; it was the first I had ever seen here. Forty miles inland, not a sign of sand, shingle or a sea breeze, or any of its companions. Yes I knew they left the coast and came inland, but I had never seen one here before. The bird was looking quite weather beaten and forlorn not the usual bright, alert bird I had seen on my excursions to the sea shore. As I watched, it let out along almost mournful piping that echoed around the rimmed bowl of water. It continued to call and after each eerie call it waited as though listening, waiting for a reply, but there was none.

Nor would there be one, the bird was alone. It had been blown many miles from its kind and now was too weak to fly and without the prospect of food the young bird was quickly running out of time. The deep water did not possess much of a shoreline. Its sharp declining edges were only briefly punctuated by an old boat slipway that formed the only entrance way into the water. How had this poor bird arrived at the pits and what lay in store for it?

As the storm blew and the waves crashed against the rocks, the air was filled with salt water spray, the flock of 40-50 oystercatchers huddled closer together. The birds on the periphery pressed in closer to the ever-tightening throng. All afternoon they had retreated up the beach as they did everyday, but today was different. The first of the winter's storms was upon them and the young birds, chicks just five months ago sensed the fear in the adults around them. The water came closer and closer. Further up the beach than it had ever done before in the young bird's short lives. The ice cold wind blew in off the sea lifting the birds feathers and tugging at their wings. The roar of the waves smashing onto the shore came at the exclusion of all other sounds. The storm was reaching its peak and the sea was getting closer. The oystercatchers squeezed closer together up against the sea wall now in an ever tightening circle until finally, there was no where else to go. If they stayed the next giant wave would claim them the only escape was up. Up into the night sky, up into the maelstrom of a storm that was to change everything for at least one young bird. The fierce wind caught hold of him the moment he took to the air, ripping it away from the others. Pushing it first one way and then twisting it another, there was no choice, the young bird did whatever the wind bid. It hurled it inland away from the sea, the oystercatcher was at its mercy and no amount of struggling against it would help. It was forced away from the only home it had known. Forced high into the waiting arms of the storm and removed from the security of the only life it had ever known.

During that first summer it had never ventured far from the constant piping of the others and the reassuring presence of the sea. The youngster's life and that of the others had been lived with the ebb and flow of the tide. Venturing down to the beach to feed as the tide receded and as the tide turned returning to roost beneath the sea wall. Waiting to repeat the same ritual over and over again. It had been a life ruled by the regularity of the sea, but now it had all changed. With no adult birds to guide it and at the whim of the storm, fear gripped the lone bird. Every time it tried to turn back it was faced with a force too strong even for its desire to return. Alone and afraid it fought an ever losing battle throughout the night. Buffeted by wind and rain it looked down upon the strange bright lights of towns and villages. The bird flew on confused and tired, staring down at the alien environment beneath his aching wings. The dawning of a new day brought with it a slight calming in the storm. As the sky grew brighter and the sun tried desperately to show itself, the oystercatcher looked down upon a completely new world. A landscape of greens and browns, of houses and trees, gone were the white tipped waves and golden sands. Confused, hungry and close to exhaustion it saw something it recognised, the first rays of sun glinting on water. Although it seemed almost still and lifeless to one who had known the moods of the ocean. It was water and water meant food, it would give it a chance to rest and regain its strength before the flight home. Down into this strange world, down past unfamiliar tree tops. Hunger now replacing fear and for the first time in fourteen long hours the bird's wings closed and it landed clumsily on to the boat slipway. Two startled mallard rose noisily into the air and after a couple of circuits overhead landed on the water on near the opposite shore. The bird knew it must feed and walked quickly down the slipway into the cold dark water. The long slender beak probing the mud and then recoiling quickly. The water tasted so strange to one who had only ever known sea water. Although different it wasn't unpleasant and the bird soon resumed the search for food along the thin ribbon of shoreline. After about twenty minutes of almost fruitless searching the bird raised its head and let out a call, hoping for a reply, a call to feed. As the minutes turned to hours the need for food became desperate, the long flight and battle with the storm had taken their toll. The young bird couldn't just wander down to a nearby mussel bed or pick along the tide line for a dead crab. It looked longingly out onto the water and saw the raft with a few gulls perched upon it. Gulls, the bird knew, greedy and argumentative gulls and what were they sat upon? It reminded the hungry bird of an easy meal it had once chanced upon. A fishing boat dragged up onto the beach, mussels that were due to be used as bait strewn all over the bottom of the boat. Yes the gulls had beaten it there, but there was enough for all. It had joined them in a feast until chased off by an angry fisherman. This would be its last chance; perhaps even now the gulls were tugging the sweet flesh from the mussel's shells. The battle with the gale had taken its toll on the young bird, summoning its last vestiges of strength; the tired and hungry bird pulled itself up into the air and flew out over the water. Its aching wings only just responding, the raft drawing closer with every wing beat. One last defiant flap enabled the bird to land clumsily on the bare wooden planks. The screeching gulls showing their annoyance and pecking at the stranger in their midst.

There were no mussels, in fact there was nothing and now with all its energy spent all that remained was to wait, wait for the end.

The oystercatcher let out a long mournful cry.

A Perfect River

Witness to our childhood
you have seen us grow
infancy, youth and adulthood
all observed by your flow

Imagine your perfect river. It will be different from mine I suppose, because rivers are like loves, personal. What one likes another may not. As I sit here writing this down I can see mine, not through the window you must understand, but by just adding together all the ingredients that would make it my perfect river.

It would have to be well hidden, away from prying eyes. No dog walkers, courting couples or playful children. I know that's a little selfish but it is my perfect river. No villages or houses looking down upon it, casting their red brick shadows where there should only be dappled green ones. I will allow one building, but in the distance and then not all of it. Just the steeple of a village church, some two or three miles away peeking over the top of a green crowned hill. That is to be it though, there must be no other intrusion, no sound of distant traffic or any other man made noise to break the spell. There must no sign of modern living, no detritus of mankind dirtying its crystal clear waters. No tin cans bobbing along disturbing the neither methodical flow, nor plastic bottles caught on overhanging boughs. Now overhanging boughs it must have, willow, oak and thorn dipping their branches. The flow causing them to nod gently as if in homage to the water. The ripples will resonate across the river and disappear into the tall water iris on the opposite shore. The bank itself should be lush and green and rising up all along it, thousands of purple flowers of loosestrife, these too should be nodding from the warm summer breeze. You see it has to be summer, well early August to be exact and hot and humid, about midday. That would be right, then I could stop and sit down on its banks. Take in, all around me. I would be able to notice the grass had been trampled down right to the waters edge and where water meets the soil I could see the cloven hoof prints. Where deer had earlier splashed their way through the shallow waters. I would be able to see the gap in the hedge on the far bank, where they pushed through on the way up to the shade of the wood on top of a distant hill. As I lay back I would be able to hear the water bubbling and boiling around a couple of large rocks in midstream that the summer water levels have exposed. A loud chirrup would draw my eyes to a kingfisher sat atop the closer of the two rocks. I would sit and watch as he waited for a minnow or just sat preening his iridescent plumage. Their would be swallows and sand martins, swooping low over the water and in the fields behind me skylarks would fill the air with song.

Where the water deepened a shoal of chub would sit and wait for a meal to come to them. Attempting and failing to take one of the huge dragonflies that seem to be everywhere. Sharing the sky are silent and graceful butterfly's, too numerous to count as they travel from flower to flower seeking out their sweet bounty. We must not forget a bridge, not a huge traffic laden concrete bridge, but a nice little arched one that maybe occasionally helps cattle to new pasture. A woodpeckers laughing call drifts down to the waters edge and is accompanied by the constant chatter of grasshoppers. A moorhen appears among some lily pads on the far bank and drifts slowly out of sight with the current. Long tendril like weeds wave with the movement of the river and combined with the midday sun, have an almost hypnotic effect as they sway first one way then another.

That would be my perfect river and I found it today.

Lucy

*A child is a gift
that we should treasure,
savour every moment,
before its gone forever*

Every so often, certain events occur in our lives and we know as soon as they happen that they will stay with us forever. They will be there throughout our lives perhaps pushed to the back of our memories, but every so often they will force themselves out and demand to be remembered. I don't mean earth shattering, life changing events, just an every day sort of moment that makes you smile and while it is taking place you know it will be there forever.

As you remember it, it will be there in the smallest detail you will be able to almost relive it. That is until the person behind you in the supermarket queue becomes increasingly concerned for your sanity and asks if you are ok, and the childlike grin disappears from your face and you get on with your life. Then it's gone until the next time you choose to remember. Well one such event happened to me this week, let me explain.

A bright sunny November day with clear blue skies and a very slight wind, just enough to convey to our nostrils that damp autumnal smell. It was warm enough not to wear a coat almost spring like in its feel I suppose. A few leaves were still hanging onto the trees and bushes, although the majority lay around our feet. There was a good crop of berries this year and the blackbirds busied themselves claiming each heavily laden bush as their own. The continuing bickering of the over zealous birds filled the air as my four year old daughter Lucy and I started on one of our many excursions, out into the countryside. As we headed down the lane she skipped off in front of me, excited by the prospect of the river in whose direction we were heading. She seemed almost liberated after a morning spent watching children's television. After a brief chase I caught up with her and we stopped briefly to pick some reed stems from the dyke that ran alongside us. The feather like silver plumes of the reeds to be used as our tickling sticks for the next ten minutes or so. It had become almost a ritual, every time we passed them. Lucy creeping up behind me and then me reacting with surprise as the reed was waved into my face or over my head. Our laughter was loud and uninhibited, as only it can be when you have no one around. We could be as loud as we wanted to be and me I could be a child again, just for a couple of hours. Our noise was not welcomed by all and we sent a kestrel screeching from his perch atop a telegraph pole. Seemingly annoyed at being disturbed, he flew low over the stubble field and decided a distant Ash tree would afford him more peace. The reeds were now forgotten, but it was not the slow quiet walk of adults, as is most children's way it had to be accompanied by a game. This time it required me to play the villain as Lucy shouted out

"What's the time Mr Wolf?"

So to the accompaniment of growls and screams we eventually reached the river. We stood awhile on the old railway bridge looking down into the clear water some fifteen feet below, swifter and deeper than usual after the recent heavy rains. Water and especially rivers have always fascinated me and I think they have cast the same spell over my daughter. Whether paddling, fishing for sticklebacks or just walking alongside them she enjoys the rivers company as I do.

Although today without our nets and too cold to paddle we would be racing sticks. Dropping them from one side of the bridge and waiting for them to re-appear out of the other. A various assortment of shapes and sizes drifting with the current and appearing the other side of the bridge with cheers of victory for the winner and jeers of derision from the loser. Each race forgotten in the search for bigger and better vessels, before even the old ones had disappeared beneath an old bent willow further down stream. The races continued for perhaps thirty minutes, Lucy totally engrossed in what she was doing. Laughing, smiling, running one way and then another, her little cheeks flushed pink with excitement. A picture to behold.

As the sun began to say goodbye we too bid our farewells to the river and began our journey home. The return trip a little more sedate our energies perhaps expended. With the river at our backs we strolled hand in hand and I began to reflect, I knew it had been a special couple of hours, but didn't really understand why. We chatted and for a while happy in the moment and each others company became quiet and for me thoughtful. I realised why it had been special. Lucy was no longer a little baby, she had started school now, a mind of her own and new friends. That afternoon she hadn't been bothered about pink shoes, hair grips or ballet class. She was with her dad and having a great time. My sons no longer came with me, friends and interests of their own that bit older and independent now. That was why it was so special because it couldn't last forever. My insecurities to the fore I gripped Lucy's hand a little tighter expecting a reassuring touch. She looked up and asked if she could whisper something to me, could she tell how I was feeling? I lowered my head and she cupped her hand to whisper in my ear.

"What's the time Mr Wolf?"

September

Not yet a time to reflect

September was upon us and with it the threat that summer was drawing to an end. Yes it was still sunny and hot, the cricket season not yet drawn to a close. Village greens remained the playground of white clad gentlemen and ladies in floral dresses busied themselves making tea in the wooden pavilions. Reds and yellows of dahlias continued to light up our gardens. The rose bushes too, hung onto the last of their blooms. House martins and swallows busied themselves feeding their young while juvenile House Sparrows searched the parched lawns for an easy meal. Yes it was still summer, but everywhere were signs that it would soon be gone for another year. Nowhere was this more obvious than down by the river. A misty morning had given way to a glorious sun filled day and I thought I would take advantage of the afternoon sun and amble gently along the bank side admiring its gentle flow. I knew September was always good for dragonflies, but I wasn't prepared for the vast waiting committee that greeted me. I would use the word plague to describe the huge numbers, but it appears less than complimentary, to what can only be described as fantastic spectacle.

From the rivers surface to the highest treetop, the air was filled with the swift darting movement of dragonflies. The slender stick like bodies flitting first one way and then another in search of both food and mates. The vast crowd of winged insects came in all sizes. From huge hawkers with a wingspan to match that of a blue tit. To the smaller but no less elegant skimmer's and darters. As well as differing in size the colours too were numerous and varied, covering all spectrums. Kingfisher blue, bright crimson red and that beautiful green you see on a peacock's tail. Even the browns seemed electric. Such colours, as if all were vying for the best carnival costume. The now brightly coloured insects a stark contrast to the uniform they had worn for the last two years, while patrolling the muddy river bed as a nymph. Now the need for camouflage had gone, for the next few weeks the sky would be theirs.

No longer did they need to take refuge from the hungry fish that had now themselves become prey. Forced into ever declining pools by the drop in water levels; they were now paying the price for the dry spring and summer. Bad news for the fish was good news for others, as is nature's way. By the old lock on a sharp bend in the river, the heron stood guard over his own personal larder. What water remained had become choked with a triffid like growth of weed, filling almost every gap, blocking out the sun and starving the remaining water of light. The reed beds stood tall along the river, following the retreat of the water, until perhaps only a two or three yards separated the opposite banks. The silver seed heads that would stay with us throughout the winter were almost unrecognisable in their purple summer guise.

All around the growing season was nearly done.

Dandelions showed their feather like globes, while the once upright nettles now hung down hoping to snare you one last time. Teasels stood tall, but dry and lifeless and the leaves on the trees no longer a bright green. The long summer days and the constant attack of insects had made them tired and sorry looking. Ash and Sycamore hung heavy with the seeds of another growing year nearly done, it would soon be time to rest. Before the rest though the dragonflies had some unfinished business.

The last rays of summer sun would be a celebration of the dragonfly.

Two Foxes

Did they know?
no harm
would come their way?

It wasn't cold, but it was raining again. Another wet and miserable day, just like it had been for the last couple of weeks. No great downpours or violent storms to empty the dark grey clouds, just a continuous drizzle. Occasionally a stiff wind would appear and threaten to blow the clouds away, but no the rain kept coming, and the wind disappeared as swiftly as it had come. Day after day we opened the curtains to be greeted by more rain. Puddles began to gather in fields, getting larger with each passing hour. Dykes that hadn't held water in years were suddenly unable to cope with what was being asked of them. Their banks spilling over into the fields to add, not to puddles, but to the pools they had become. These new bodies of water attracted mallards to their shores, and they presented a forlorn and confused picture, as they paddled around in the ever deepening water. All this where only a few months previously the corn had been ripening in the heat of the summer sun. Willow herb and harebell had been sharing the hedgerow with brightly coloured butterflies. All that now seemed like a distant memory, as the rain seemed to have penetrated into every last dry sanctuary, and a grey melancholy had settled on the land. The tide had made its way into the woods, dripping down along the branches and onto the woodland floor. Even the normally impenetrable barrier of the conifers had been breached. As I strolled or I suppose splashed would be a better word, through the trees. I marvelled at the vast array of fungi that had decided it was now time to appear. As if by magic, where two days previously there had been no sign, they now seemed to be everywhere.

I named the ones I knew and marvelled and guessed at those I didn't. Shaggy ink cap, stinkhorn and pink wood blewitt adorned the ground while up among the trees I noticed honey fungus, oyster fungus and the sulphur polypore. The damp had been just the trigger this little bit of nature required.

Leaving the dark of the woods into what seemed a bright afternoon that was until my eyes adjusted, and I realised it was still the same grey afternoon that I had left home in. I turned right up a gently rising slope and along a muddy farm track. The sticky glutinous mud hung onto my boots and refused to budge, as I leapt from side to side of the track trying to avoid the deepest of the puddles. Although that was guess work and each boot took on the colour of the surrounding fields. A small group of Redwings squabbled over the last few hawthorn berries in the hedgerow and then noticing me, left with a loud chattering, annoyed at the interruption to their non- stop search for food. As they departed a chaffinch saw its chance and quickly took the opportunity of a meal, replacing the Redwings hurried gorging with an almost delicate refined feeding ritual. It too was aware of me, but a little less concerned and continued to feed as I passed by, until himself evicted by the returning Redwings, once I was a safe distance away. The chaffinch made his way into the woods in search of a drier and perhaps easier meal. I turned with the intention of continuing my journey but was stopped in my tracks almost immediately. In front of me and walking straight towards me not fifteen yards away, were two of the scruffiest mangy looking foxes I had ever seen. They both looked damp and bedraggled, their heads bowed and their ears almost flat to their heads. Their normally brilliant white bibs were stained with grey patches which had smeared onto their chestnut brown coats. The mud had coloured their legs and hid from me the white tips of their tails. They were not particularly big foxes perhaps this years young, although one was little larger than the other and was leading the way. As they got closer to within only a few feet, the larger of the two raised his head and saw me. I waited for them to break into a run, to rush off into the nearest cover, but no. Without even breaking stride it turned almost nonchalantly and led its companion towards the wood and away from me. No urgency in its step just the same steady pace. It all seemed a little surreal, every fox I had ever seen before was so alert and quick and I had certainly never been that close to one before. These two seemed somehow wrong, tired and lifeless.

I didn't attempt to follow, I just stood and watched their haunches disappear into the darkness of the woods and was left wondering why. Why hadn't they seen me earlier? Why were they so dirty and lifeless? Why were they together and why didn't they run when they saw me?

Usually a solitary animal out of the breeding season had these two shared the same mishap. Were they to share the same fate? I shook myself from my thoughts and peered into the wood. They had gone, they had disappeared. Even now though I can still see those two cold lifeless eyes as the larger of the two foxes looked up at me. I wonder what became of them.

White and Green

Stop and ask why

Two colours, on their own beautiful and fresh but together and at that moment, inspirational.

White and green, a brilliant clean white, unsullied and pure and a vibrant emerald green, alive and vivid. It would have made a magnificent painting or a film, set to classical music, perhaps a Viennese waltz. That would have been fitting the white feather twisting and turning. The slightest breath of the warm spring breeze changing its direction, speeding it up and slowing it down. Sometimes spiralling as it glided across the crystal clear waters at the whim of the breeze. As white as any January snowdrop and as welcome a sight.

Then there was the green, all around the fresh new growth both above and beneath the water. Grass and young nettles pushing forth into a bright new world, released from its wintry grip. Beneath the slow moving shallow water could be seen the long tendril like weeds, swaying as if one with the current.

As the feather danced along I mused at the coincidence that had brought these two colours together, or is coincidence too easy a word to use. It just puts things together in the same place at the same time, without an explanation. Ten minutes later leaving home and I would have missed the whole thing, as the feather got caught up in some overhanging branches, along with a couple of plastic bottles and a tennis ball. What if the swan whose feather it was had chosen to nest further up stream away from the footpath? Or like one of its winter companions had succumbed to one of the overhead cables that criss-crosses the fields? What if the breeze hadn't snatched that feather from her bill, as she had been lining her nest?

Or was she stretching and preening after a long spell sat nursing her brood? Maybe it owed its presence to some sort of territorial dispute, whatever reason it wasn't just there. And that was only the white.

What had made the green so much brighter in this part of the river? Was it just the new growth, or the bright Spring day? The clear water or just my heightened senses as I too felt the departure of winter. The bank side vegetation always grew tall and dense here, as did the weeds in the river. In fact by the end of summer this bend in the river always became clogged with plant life, and the water almost came to a standstill. As I listened the distant growling of a tractor, gave me perhaps the reason for this accelerated growth.

Every year in the spring the farmer sprayed his fields, and I had watched him on many occasions on this particular field. He started at the top of the slope and worked his way down towards the river. As he turned for the upward slope, the huge spraying arm flicked out over the river and deposited a nutrient rich cocktail into the water, along the whole length of the field. Perhaps twice a year every year the river and bankside plants were given an unneeded boost. Maybe that was why it was so green. That was why the feather was so defined against its background.

Yes I could have reached down into the water and taken that feather into my hand, the only sensation felt would have been the cold water. I could have gazed upon its beauty at close hand, but no the beauty was the moment. To take it would have removed its majesty, it would have become limp and lifeless, just a feather. As I watched

It disappear the moment took on a greater importance; I may never be privileged to witness that fragile elegance again. It was a moment to savour, but not a coincidence.

They Missed Out

Away for the winter
are you sure

The Tree creeper, so small and vulnerable. Scurrying in and out of the ivy that seemed to be strangling the life out the aged ash tree. How could this tiny bird survive five long months of an English winter? Maybe its insignificance was its saviour. Could the cold icy wind be bothered to search out and find this little bird? Was it that inconspicuous that winter just forgot about it? After all it was easy to miss as it went about its business, unnoticed by almost everyone who passed it by that winter. Not looking about them as they rushed by, pulling up their collars and quickening their pace. The lure of a centrally heated home beckoned them. Well they missed out because I stayed awhile and watched.

I watched as the little brown bird went its way, checking beneath the leaves of ivy and looking between the deep fissures in the bark. Its tiny scimitar like bill probing the smallest of gaps for sustenance. The time of plenty had passed and the next few months would be a constant battle to survive. It was too engrossed in its search for food to notice me. As the tiny bird forged its way in a spiral up the tree, I thought how it so obviously resembled its old country name of tree mouse. His mottled brown body blending perfectly with the bark of the tree. In fact if it had kept still, I may have passed it by myself. Its busy lifestyle demanded it was constantly on the move and that was what gave its presence away. I noticed a slight movement and then another, as it reappeared from around the other side of the trunk. There was no mistake, a silvery eye stripe and the tail pushed into the tree to aid its acrobatics. It looked just like a mouse as it wound its way up the tree. Stopping briefly to feed and quickly off again, all the time alert, not wanting to miss anything that may be a meal. As I watched, it became so obvious that this little bird was so suited to the niche it had chosen. The long claws offering a grip that could not be broken, the bill seeking out food that no other bird could access. Yes it would last the winter because nature had made it that way. Eventually after about twenty minutes and three ascents of the tree, it decided it had investigated every nook and cranny and it flew off to start the process all over again.

The tree now became still and lifeless without its little companion, but it still it held my attention. I stood and admired its stark majesty, against the rapidly darkening sky. The bare branches shorn of their coat of green held next year's leaves tightly in jet black buds. The tree was waiting for the warmth to return and days to lengthen, but until then it would remain still and lifeless. Except that is for the odd bird who chose to pay a visit.

Herald of Summer

Here for a while unannounced,
but for its own fanfare
Gone for a while unannounced,
oh for the missing fanfare

There it was the herald of summer, that promise of longer and brighter days to come. The prospect of warm sunny days and clear blue skies, filled with swallows and butterflies. I had been waiting and listening for a couple of weeks now thinking maybe, this was the year it would not return. Maybe that long journey from east Africa had taken its toll, or perhaps a storm had blown it to pastures new. It just seemed a little late this year, it was already April 28th and it had usually set up its territory by now. It's monotonous call sounding from atop the huge poplar tree, *"cuckoo, cuckoo".* The sound filling the trees and surrounding countryside. Announcing its arrival to all. A few swallows and even a single swift had shown themselves and been busy searching out food. Then there was the House Martins, well they had arrived en masse about a week ago now. Appearing and disappearing as the frequent spring showers threatened to make us forget about the forthcoming summer. The majority of trees though were still bare with only a few brave buds yet prepared to give way to the inevitable.

My path to the Poplar tree meant I had to come round a right angled bend before I would be able to find my quarry. So I heard it long before I saw it, as was usually the scenario. The constant call getting louder as I neared the bend in the track, the expectation growing with every step. I knew where to look and was looking forward to seeing my old friend. Who I presumed was not so keen to renew our friendship. As soon as I rounded the bend the cuckoo took to the air, its fast shallow wing beats giving the look of a sparrow hawk. There was no mistake though, its pointed wings and pale breast showed it to be what I had waited to see. It flew the short distance to a telegraph wire and decided the distance between us was now quite sufficient, and so carried on with the plaintive call *"cuckoo cuckoo"*. I too was happy with the distance between us, as I could use my binoculars to study the bird without it fleeing at the slightest movement from me.

There it sat looking most uncomfortable as though it would fall to the ground at any moment; in fact that was perhaps one of my earliest childhood identification signs for a cuckoo. If it looked like it was going to fall off its perch, it was one. Its long tail cocked sky ward's in an uneven balancing act. Its equally long wings extending almost to its tail giving it a most unusual stance. The slate grey upperparts highlighting the bright piercing yellow eye that seemed to be watching me. The breast was a pure white with dark bars running across it reminding me of the archetypical burglar's garb. How apt then, as soon the cuckoo would be visiting nests, while the true occupants were away. Unlike the burglar though the cuckoo would replace the valuables it took. It would leave a single egg, matching almost exactly in colour with those already in the nest. This would mean a long and busy summer for the foster parents, as they busied themselves supplying between five and six hundred meals a day, to the ever-open gape of the young chick.

A sedge warbler sent forth his sweet melody into the air, and a couple of whitethroats were singing lustily from the same perch as the cuckoo. As their name suggests the white of their underparts contrasted sharply with the rusty red of their wings. As they finished advertising their whereabouts, they disappeared into the thick tangle of brambles below. I felt sure the cuckoo was watching and waiting, for their next excursion, from the now visible nest. I knew then the cuckoos summer had begun.

As I turned to leave the cuckoo began to call, *"cuckoo cuckoo"* and I felt quite relieved. Summer would be coming after all and I looked forward to seeing the harbinger of it for the next few months.

A Long Hot Summer

A long time coming
with her warm sweet air
three whole seasons
waiting for her to reappear

The summer went on and on, one heat filled day blurring into the next. The sound and feel of rain seemed but a distant memory. The sort of thing that only happened on cold winter days, which during this sun soaked summer, seemed a million miles away. So as the sun shone and the countryside wilted under its gaze. I began to notice for the first time in my short life, the changing of the seasons. From the gently lengthening days of spring to those long hot Summer days. The fact that it was the hottest summer on record meant nothing to a young boy. It would be a few years before I realised that not every English summer was filled with the clear blue cloudless skies of this one. The crops ripened early and by the beginning of August even the farmers had slowed down. The mad dash to get in the harvest became more of a steady methodical march, of men who knew there would be no change in the weather. Cattle seemed uninterested in grazing the dusty brown grass, and sought shade beneath the boughs of the old chestnut trees, which they shared with the local Roe deer. The trees themselves were clinging on, sending out their roots into the hard compact soil in search of the remaining moisture. As evening approached and the temperature dropped a little. The cattle lazily strolled down to the river, to drink and perhaps find something to eat as the last vestiges of green had managed to hang on to the bankside.

Throughout the summer the river had slowed and as time wore on into September, it gradually came to a standstill. The water though hung on for a while in ever diminishing pools, until eventually only the odd one remained. Full of movement these pools contained the last of the fish thrashing about, trying desperately to extract the last of the oxygen from the brackish water, before the inevitable happened. Only a few months earlier, their smooth torpedo like bodies could be seen breaking the rivers surface to take unsuspecting Mayfly. Now the rainbow trout themselves had become the prey. Herons came and gorged themselves. Usually a solitary hunting bird they forgot their inhibitions, not realising that this would be their last meal from this river for a few years. The Kingfisher sat forlornly looking more in hope than anticipation for any minnows he may have missed. He too would soon be moving on, just as the swans had already done. Then just as October and relief beckoned, the water had gone. There was no longer a river, just an open wound. Filled with ever widening cracks, that challenged any passing clouds to try and attempt to return the river to its former glory.

Although the summer seemed to last forever, late autumn brought with it rain. A whole summers worth of rain seemed to fall in just a few short weeks. Once the surrounding fields had taken their fill, it was the turn of the river. The cracks began to close and small pools began to form. As the rain continued to fall, these pools began to join together. The river began to regain a little of its elegance and then even a gentle flow. The river was coming back to life.

As winter came and a new year began it seemed as if that long hot summer would be just a memory, until you looked closely. Yes the river ran clear and swift, but the fish were gone so too were the herons and kingfishers. Where once the bottom of the river had been filled with lush green growth it now showed itself to be sandy and devoid of life. Yes the river was flowing again but it would be a few more years before the scars healed completely.

Hero

A man admired for admirable achievements or qualities

Terrington marsh sits at the edge of the wash at the mouth of the river Nene. The high grassed sea banks marking its boundary. Where rural tamed Lincolnshire becomes wild and ancient salt marsh takes over. So unlike any other landscape I was familiar with, and I wondered what I might find to give me some sort of affinity with it.

Let me explain. I needed that affinity, that feeling of familiarity. It was to be a place of beauty, of distant horizons, remoteness and wildlife. If it had been good enough to inspire Sir Peter Scott, it had to do something for me. His writings had always given me great enjoyment and fed my love of the great outdoors. In amongst those pages I could see the red skies and huge flocks of noisy honking geese. His delicate paintings showed a man who was in his element and at one with it. As a child the calls from the pages would keep me from sleep, for just one more page. Calling me one day to seek out this wilderness, and hope not too much had changed, since his time here.

Where to start, only one place really. It had to be where it had all began for him, where he had begun a lot of his forays out into the marsh and that was his home. In amongst those yellowing pages, it shone out like the beacon it was meant to be. A simple sketch at the top of the page, a white lighthouse. One of a pair built on the banks of the river, meant as a folly rather than an aid to shipping. A sign to Mother Nature that man was here in this, one of her last English wildernesses and she would be tamed. A strange place then for a conservationist to call home. So this was his home and studio for 6 years from 1933-39, and now it stood in front of me, proud and defiant. A white citadel shining brightly in the summer sun.

Pointing up out of the sea of green that surrounded it, and looking over the chocolate brown river that flowed swiftly alongside it. Lifted straight from the pages of the book and placed down in front of me. There were no huge extensions or glass conservatories attached to its side. No signs advertising tea and ice cream, just a single brass plaque paying homage to the great man. The eighty or so years had been good to his home, yes a few coats of whitewash had been applied, but as far as I was concerned I was seeing it as he had. An escape, an oasis, a place to lose yourself, or perhaps find yourself. Had it changed that little or was it me willing it not to have done?

Looking down at my ordnance survey map so devoid of contour lines. I noticed the sea bank I intended to walk along; 200 yards from the lighthouse it turned almost 90 degrees to face the sea, its timeless foe. There printed on the shore right in my path was the date 1951. Until that date the high tides had ebbed at the great mans front door. So change had come, but maybe the gate I found myself climbing over he too had climbed. Then like me, armed with binoculars and rucksack, he had sought the solitude and freedom of the marsh. Unlike me, he may have found it. My first few steps were accompanied by the loud roar of jet engines, as a continual flow of aircraft left me unable to hear the wind in the grass. Then I remembered he too must have had to put up with the occasional intrusion, as an ill equipped Britain decided a little too late, to prepare them for its second great war of the twentieth century. Aircraft too would have filled his skies and he would answer that call to arms and bid his home goodbye. As the aircraft disappeared out to sea I too left the lighthouse behind, and as I walked I could feel the warm July sun on my face. The breeze blowing off the marsh brought with it the smell of the sea, urging me to step down from the grassy bank and seek out its source. Pleading with me to find a way through the winding creeks and muddy pools, out past the emerald green banks of sapphire and onto the golden sands that shimmered in the distant heat haze.

There lay the seals unconcerned by all around them basking in the midday sun. Not even aware that I was squinting through my binoculars at them. I walked on, the view unchanging. On my left the green gold and blue of first marsh and then beach with the blue sea and sky drifting off to infinity. On my right miles of hedge less fields of barley and wheat, just waiting for a couple more weeks of sunshine to signal the beginning of the harvest. Over in the distance the flat top towers of fenland churches gave away the location of villages. Above all of this, a huge cloudless blue

sky, that stretched from one horizon on my right, over my head and all the way down to the other on my left. That was it, I think I had it, I think I understood. Yes he had his birds and his love of the sea helped tie him to this place, and maybe that was just it, but I don't think so. Beneath the huge sky in the middle of this featureless landscape, you know your place, you realise how small a part you play and how really insignificant you are. I thought about this as I turned and wandered back to my car. Climbing back over the gate and beginning to think of home, it was easier to see why the great man had loved this place. And as I bid it farewell I was sure I could here the sea calling me back.

Trees

Giants among us

There they stand almost unnoticed, some tall and proud others aged and bent. Yes we see them but do we really pay them any attention, or do we just take them for granted? They have always been there, but in different guises. Everyday they play a little part in our lives, without us perhaps even realising. Yes there are the obvious times. A balmy summer's day spent beneath a fully clothed sycamore, and the stark majesty of a naked oak against a storm lashed winters sky.

All seeing trees, do you ever stop and think about them, or even spend a bit of time just looking at them, because I'm pretty sure they do us. They observe and play a great part in most of our lives, but are we aware of it.

As babies our proud parents wheeled us along tree lined suburban avenues, and then left us to kick off our blankets beneath the dappled shade of the silver birch, at the bottom of the garden. As infants we marvelled at the vast size of the giants around us and kicked gaily at there fallen autumn finery. Then as children we clambered among their branches and ran beneath their boughs, as the local woodland became a playground for our adventures. Even now as adults we admire their longevity, we appreciate their autumn colours and if we stop our busy lives for a moment they can help us remember.

Perhaps that perfect days fishing beneath an overhanging willow, or that ferocious downpour that we witnessed from beneath a huge Horse Chestnut. Maybe that first kiss stolen behind that cherry tree in the playground, or just an old apple tree at the bottom of our grandparent's garden. All of us have memory of a tree, just think about it.

The Halcyon Bird

Great and mighty hunter,
where have you been
I saw you once from afar
as though in a dream.

A flash of bright metallic blue, speeding away from us. Lightning fast towards the nearest bend in the river. That's all that most of us will ever see of a kingfisher, and that's if we are lucky. That beautiful almost tropical bird that is the measure of the well- being of our streams and rivers. One day though I was lucky.

It began just the same as any other day, with the same view I always got, as I walked alongside the river. No matter how quiet or careful I approached, what I presumed was a favoured fishing spot. I only ever saw my usual 4-5 seconds vision of my elusive quarry. Just enough time to raise my binoculars to my eyes and watch him disappear under the old railway bridge, and so out of sight. Yes, I had seen kingfishers in other places along the river, but always the same, just enough time to see the glint of the sun on their electric blue back. Enough time to see the bright orange chest and maybe, make out the long black beak. I saw this every time I chanced upon them, but I wanted more. I wanted to see them dive and re-appear with a minnow. To watch them rest and preen their iridescent coat. Just be privileged to spend more than 4 or 5 seconds in their company. I usually sat around and waited, convinced they would return, but it always proved to be a pointless endeavour. On this particular day though I didn't even bother to wait. The weather was a bit changeable; the bright sunshine of the morning was soon to be replaced by a dark threatening sky, blowing

in from the north. Discretion got the better of me and I decided to head home before I got caught in the forthcoming rain.

Heading downstream towards the dry stone wall that formed my gateway to the open fields, which in turn would lead me home. My rush was halted by a group of long tailed tits flitting amongst a stand of alders, which overhung the river. They chatted amongst themselves, their high pitched rippling calls seeming to fill the branches. These delightful little birds had always been a favourite of mine, ever since I became aware of their existence as a child. So I settled myself down on a long ago fallen tree, to watch those accommodating little creatures, in their never ending search for food. These little birds seemed too fragile to cope with a strong wind, as though the slightest gust would send them tumbling from their perches and out over the open fields. I suppose the best way to describe a long tailed tit is like a little ball of cotton wool with an exceedingly long tail protruding from it. The tiny beaks, but a pin prick on their white face. How could such a small mouth take in enough food to sustain their busy little lives? But not only had they survived but flourished, until an outing did not seem complete without the accompaniment of these little rotund white, pink and black companions. An orange comma butterfly passed them by, seeming almost a giant in comparison. Its neatly scalloped wings and mottled markings visible as it drifted down, passing only inches from my face.

While I sat engrossed in both the butterflies and the bird's antics, the sky had got darker, and too late I noticed as the first few drops of rain started to fall, forming patterns on the rivers surface. The coming of the rain was the signal for my busy little companions to flee and seek shelter. Those first few drops soon became a downpour, and I too looked around for cover. The dark clouds had promised rain and lots of it. The rain quickly got heavier and heavier, until the shower became a torrent. The river began to hiss and boil, as the clouds above added to its flow and refused to yield. I pushed myself back against an old hawthorn bush, hoping its canopy would protect me from the worst of the downpour. Now alone I sat and waited. It was to be a long wait, yes it eased a little but only a little, and I was getting soaked. As my shelter became saturated so to did I. My clothes put up a brief struggle, but the raindrops worked their way through the tangled web of leaves and branches, then down onto me. Leaving me feeling most uncomfortable and more than a little chilly.

I would like to say I was just on the point of making a run for home, but no I had settled into my position, with my back pushed up against

Rain Watching

Little drops of life

Soft and gentle rain, forming intertwining circles on the surface of the river. Silent and secretive, if it wasn't for the ripples on the rivers surface you would not have even noticed the rain. It's not proper rain; even the sky's not sure what's going on. It's still blue and the only clouds in sight are the white fluffy ones we associate with summer picnics. In fact it's a mystery where it has come from at all. Then it stops, just as suddenly as it started and there is nothing to show it was ever there. Until perhaps you glimpse the silver like beads hanging from a spiders web, that adorns the gate in front of you. That is my favourite sort of rain, but I only ever seem to see it in the spring, just before the leaves are open and maybe that's why I like it.

Of course there are other types of rain. The huge downpour that is accompanied by a strong wind that bends the trees and causes everyone and everything to seek shelter. Rain pouring down in never ending sheets, the sky darkening until daytime is replaced by a strange half- light that lends a sense of foreboding to the occasion. The rain finding its way into every nook and cranny. A drip becomes a trickle and a trickle a torrent, until drains and gutters give up the fight. Great for rain watching, but through a window maybe best.

Then there is the summer shower. One minute blinding sunshine, the clear blue sky filled with bird song and the last thing on anyone's mind is rain. Then you notice the birds have gone and before you have time to bring it to someone's attention, a great roll of thunder announces the arrival of a deluge. It sends you scurrying to bring in the washing and pack away the children's toys. Then as you reach the refuge of your house, you stop and look back and it's gone, as quickly as it came. The patio has already started to dry and the sky is full of bird song again.

Now rain at night can be almost mysterious. The rain drops taking on a strange orange glow as the street light highlights their downward path. Stopping off to tap on our bedroom windows just to let us know they will be waiting for us in the morning.

Then of course there is drizzle, not soft rain, not hard rain, but continuous rain. Everywhere seems grey, and your mood begins to match its surroundings. You can't go anywhere without a coat. Your eyes constantly scan the sky for a little piece of blue, that will signal a change in the weather, but no, just grey. Puddles getting bigger by the minute and beginning to resemble small ponds. An excursion from home becomes an exercise in damp avoidance. Yes it's great for ducks and for children too, who don their macs and multi-coloured wellingtons and wile away the hours splashing, but it's not for me.

I like that soft gentle rain that only seems to happen on spring days.

Look Next Time

In the darkest moments
something will be shining
It just needs seeking out

The sunlight filtered through the cold autumn air. Working its way past the tree tops, down through the lower branches and stopping to dance on the woodland floor. On its way down it had played among the dark spiky fingers of a blackthorn bush and picked out the delicate threads of gossamer of a spider's web. The suns rays reflecting off its almost silk like texture, making it seem like the finest silver thread, worthy of only the grandest garment. But here it was running from one bare twig to another an almost perfect symmetrical pattern. Moving slightly in the cold breeze that had somehow penetrated the wood on this cold autumn morning. Threatening to snap apart at any moment, but not doing so. Its fragile beauty belying its strength. It was sharing the bush with the last few sloes, which had lost their colour and begun to wrinkle and dry as if in protest at being left behind, to face the winter alone. These remaining sloes had been missed by a group of noisy thrushes the previous day. They had blundered their way clumsily through the bush, ripping apart the spider's web. Leaving only a couple of strands hanging limply down. As soon as the hungry birds had passed, the spider appeared and began to repair its lair. Starting from exactly the same place as before, an almost identical web appeared in less than a couple of hours. That very same web, now grabbed my attention. A small piece of beauty on a bleak, damp afternoon. Easily missed, but once seen never forgotten.

A Different Kind Of Jewel

Jewels we crave to lock away
To keep and occasionally show
The real jewels are there for us all to see
But only if you look and know

Right down in the bottom left hand corner of Wales I found a jewel. A bright sparkling jewel, that brought a smile to my face and a spring to my step. A thing of beauty and resonance that I had very rarely seen, and like all jewels it looked its best with the sun shining upon it. Different shades and hues radiated from it, lighting up not just my spirit, but lifting my mood and producing a knowing smile. It was no ordinary jewel, no ruby or sapphire, no string of pearls or elegantly fashioned diamond ring. No you couldn't take it in your hands and deny others the chance to see it. You couldn't lock it away and set it free at your whim. I'm sure others have seen it, but maybe not as I did and I don't think it would ever look the same for me again. It was like your first love, never to be forgotten. It would always be remembered as I saw it that first time, that early August morning. Those first two hours we spent alone together.

I suppose it was about 7.30 when I left the cottage, a little shaft of sunshine had made its way through the trees and climbing roses that hung over the windows. Then pushed between a gap in the curtains and crept its way through the bedroom and decided it was time that I woke. Nudging me, urging me to rise and go and join it. It demanded my attention, so brushing off my lack of sleep I rose and dressed quickly. As I exited from the cottage each sound seemed magnified as I tried not to wake anyone. Closing the creaking front door behind me, I was greeted by bright sunshine and a cloudless powder blue sky, that promised a magnificent summer's day ahead.

Underfoot the grass of the garden path was still heavily laden with the glistening dew that tends to linger at that time of year. By the gateway as if crafted in secret overnight, a couple of small toadstools had appeared and I carefully stepped over them, not wishing to destroy their delicate beauty. I slipped out through the gate and into the lane. I had driven down this lane not five hours since, in the dark of night. I was now eager to see what it held, as the day shift had taken over from the lone fox which had observed our arrival in the early hours of the morning. To this our holiday home for the next week. That quaint little cottage, by the coast, on the outskirts of a tiny hamlet, at the end of a winding lane.

Now lane is such a better word than road and we should not use it lightly. It conjures up such images of the English countryside. Of hedgerows, and flowers of tall grass and bright sunshine. Of blackberries and butterflies, yes this was a lane. I don't think it travelled fifty yards without twisting, first one way and then another. Each blind bend offered the promise of stumbling across some hidden secret. As all lanes should be it was narrow and lined on both sides by tall hedgerows. Every so often huge, handsome trees rose majestically alongside and above it. The hedges were ancient and dense, so dense that they concealed all that lay behind them. So that gateways to this secret world were eagerly sought.

As soon as I closed the gate behind me I knew I was in for a treat. The telegraph wires that ran from the cottage hung down heavily with a large gathering of juvenile swallows, who sat chattering among themselves. Perhaps discussing their impending departure. Honeysuckle still flowered in the upper reaches of the hedgerow, and its heady scent drifted down to meet me and draw me along the lane. Another step and another surprise, as a large bottle green dragonfly darted past my nose, its busy wings disturbing the still, warm air. Another creature of the sky, a Greater Spotted Woodpecker drummed noisily somewhere up ahead of me. Then as I rounded the bend, my arrival disturbed him and put him to flight. His silhouette leaving the trunk of a large sycamore tree on my left and flitting across the field to alight upon another, not thirty yards away. His quick undulating flight certain give away that it was a Woodpecker, to even the most unaccomplished watcher. I stopped briefly at a gateway and rested upon it. I stood and watched the black and white bird work its way up the tree, until finally it disappeared into the leafy crown. And there I stood a while longer, just listening; it was that sort of day. It wasn't quiet, but the only sounds you could here were worth listening to. Singing birds, buzzing bees and a couple of grasshoppers seemed to be having a tête-à-tête, just perfect. You could even hear the cows chewing the grass. A steady rhythmical grinding, as they slowly manoeuvred their great lumbering bodies, across the emerald green carpet that purported to be a field.

So to the next bend, and a loud piercing *keoo* brought my eyes up to the sky, as a buzzard circled. His large frame gliding effortlessly up into the air. Wheeling its way higher and higher on the warming thermals with hardly a wing beat, and calling all the time. I continued to hear its mournful cry long after it had drifted out of sight, into the glare of the now blinding sun. Already I was smitten, what more could this place hold?

I continued on, purple loosestrife and harts tongue ferns pushed out from the hedge bottom. A movement amongst the latters shining leaves, showed to me a toad seeking shade from the days rising temperature. At every bend rabbits flung themselves into their burrows, not turning to see the unwelcome guest, marvel at their speed and agility. Along one of the fields a track rose steeply up to a wood and there I spied a hare. He watched me diligently as I passed him by, on my journey along a man made highway that nature seemed to have allowed. Just as a reminder of whose territory this really was, tufts of grass sprung up from beneath the tarmac. Perhaps a battle the grass could not win, but a reminder as to how enduring Mother Nature can be.

The hedgerows were already hanging heavy with the fruit of a summers labours, promising a bumper harvest. Cob nuts had begun to fall and now lay strewn across the floor, accompanied by a few not yet ripe acorns. The source of the acorns stood above me, a vast oak tree whose branches spanned the lane casting a heavy dark shadow down onto me. As I stared in to its higher echelons, I noticed what I first took to be a child's ball. Only when I coupled it with a soft buzzing sound did I realise it to be a wasp's nest. Hanging precariously from the thinnest of branches, and all around wasps were beginning their days work, as their summer of toil drew to an end. As I left the shade of the oak and stepped back out into the sun, two speckled wood butterflies danced in front of me in an almost ballerina type fashion. Birdsong filled the air and a Spotted Flycatcher appeared and disappeared just as quickly, as is their way. It was perfect each twist and turn of the lane was now treated with trepidation. Surely soon I would spy a car speeding towards me, a tin can or a discarded crisp packet. Surely this utopia couldn't go on, and it didn't.

Although it didn't end in a hail of engine noise or an overflowing rubbish bin. The lane began to descend, only a slight incline hardly noticeable really, until the last thirty or forty yards. Here it plunged down and my eyes were met with a magnificent vista. After being hemmed in, my course chosen for me by the lane, this was the grand finale.

A huge expanse of sapphire blue water with emerald green grassy banks, covered with white ox eye daises and blue chicory flowers, stood before me. As well as the best nature had to offer, atop the grassy bank, the other side of the water sat a ruined castle. Not a hundred yards away across the water, the crumbling ramparts and towers were ringing with the call of jackdaws. Yes it was the end but what a way to end. A beautiful, magical view on any day, but today it was another facet to my jewel. That little lane in the bottom left hand corner of Wales.

Not What I Expected

If it's not what you seek
does that make it not worth the wait?
So hold your breath and sit awhile
does it matter if you are late?

It was already getting late when I arrived; I suppose it was about 3.30, as I pulled my car onto the side of the road. I put on my gloves, coat and hat, shut the car door and set off. For what I hoped was going to be a very rewarding hour and a half of twilight. I had received a phone call from a friend the previous evening, to tell me he had seen a Barn Owl in the very location to which I was now eagerly heading. It was a short car ride from my house, then a ten minute walk through the woods, too good a chance to miss. The woodland was quite dense and overgrown, a mix of both deciduous and coniferous trees, with a clear slow moving river running through it. Where the river left the woods the landscape opened up to reveal large fields and deep water filled dykes. Most of the fields had recently been ploughed, but two of them, down by a small copse had been left. The farmer left these every year, as rough grassland over the winter and this is where I was heading. As it was early January, the sun had not ventured too high during the day, and consequently the temperature had not got much above freezing. Puddles from the night before had kept their thin coat of ice, as the sun had failed to find them tucked away beneath trees, and in dark shady corners. Fallen autumn leaves also remained crisp and white. And now as the short winter's day began to draw to a close, I felt the chill air on my face and watched as my warm breath rose up in a vapour in front me. I hurried along the river bank stopping only briefly to admire a Grey Wagtail at the waters edge. The incessant banter of rival pheasants greeted me as I entered the woods, their calls travelled far into the air as they began to take to their roosting perches, in the lower branches of the trees.

Day time was fading quickly. Out of the woods I made my way quickly across the grass to a little wooden bridge which crossed a dyke. The exact same spot my friend had seen the Barn Owl the previous night and this would be my vantage point also. As I settled myself down to wait the sky was already beginning to change its shade. The darkening blue of the afternoon being replaced by a soft pink, as the sun began to sink behind the dark skeletal trees. So in anticipation I waited and I waited, and it got colder and it got colder. As the temperature dropped the sky became less pink and more red. It bathed everything in a warm rosy glow and belied the dropping temperature, but still no owl. Three Roe deer skipped across in front of me, about twenty yards away too busy with each other to notice me as they made their way into the woods for the night. Their little white tails flicking as they disappeared into the darkness of the trees. There were also a couple of herons sparring with each other on the edge of a ploughed field. Taking it in turns to leap a few feet into the air, then as they landed they snapped at each other with their long pointed bills. For some reason they put me in mind of a couple of trainee ballerinas practicing their moves, as first one then the other took to the air almost in slow motion. Landing awkwardly on those long gangly legs, with their huge dark wings outstretched. Amusing though it was, this was not what I had come to see and as the light was fading and with my ears and finger tips beginning to feel decidedly uncomfortable. I decided to make my way along the hedgerow and see if the owl was patrolling the other side of the copse. I hadn't gone more than two steps when a frantic flapping erupted from beneath my feet, sending a cold chill through my body. A dark silhouette flapped speedily away from me and into the copse. By its silhouette, and manic call, I recognised it as a Woodcock. I had been stood just two yards away from it. For perhaps forty minutes, and I was completely unaware of it.

The sudden noise had managed to shake me from an almost trance like state, that seemed to have enveloped me, as I had stood quietly waiting. My senses quickly returned and I realized how cold I had become. Like the woodcock it was my time to depart. The reds and the pinks of the afternoon had now been replaced by an ever-darkening sky, so I turned and I headed for my car. As I trudged through the quickly freezing air, the grass crunching beneath my feet, I began to wonder if from a lofty perch, the Barn Owl was now ready to hunt. Now the intruder into its world had gone.

The Watcher

Our special place it will be
always there for you and me
all around there will be change
but I will seek and there you will be

Slowly it fell, taking its time, turning first one way and then another. There was no hurry, it even stopped briefly and rested on a gnarled old limb. That is until a gentle breath of wind sent it tumbling on its way again. Floating down to join its companions already lying thickly on the grass below. An ever growing carpet of reds, gold's and browns. Soon to be joined by the still green leaves of the Ash, retaining their colour as if in protest at their all too short a growing season. The last of whose buds had burst only come with the onset of June. Now as October neared its conclusion, the carpet of leaves had nearly covered completely the ground beneath the trees. The storm of the previous day had turned a steady trickle into a cascade. The wind ripping all but the most stubborn of the autumn leaves away from the branches and twigs, they had adorned all summer. A multitude of colours and shapes, falling to the ground as another growing season had reached an end. All summer long the tree had stood at the edge of the wood, just as it had done for the last one hundred and twenty years. Looking out over the open grassland down to the river, and beyond to the village that lay in the valley. A single Sycamore amongst all those Ash, Oak, Elm and Beech. One sycamore among perhaps two thousand trees surely it had a story to tell.

It had not been planted with the others by the estate workers, all those years ago, but had found its own way to the lofty mount a couple of years later. A single wind blown seed brought to rest by an autumn storm. Its parentage long forgotten, as the gales blew it far from the reach of its kin. As the winds calmed the sycamore key fell to the ground and nestled itself down into the loose soil of a not long abandoned rabbits burrow. As winter came it lay undisturbed, not taken by the hungry beaks of birds and even passed over by the inquisitive nostrils of a badger. As the large mammal had rooted for roots and worms, it had unwittingly sealed our seed beneath the few inches of soil it needed to survive the harshest of the winter weather. As spring arrived and the race for new life began, the warming soil, and a sudden downpour nudged our seed to germinate, reminded it of its reason. The initial struggle to break free from its casing, and join every living thing on the hillside in a race for survival, had begun. It forced its way up through the soil fighting to catch up with the others, already three years in advance of it, and with ever widening trunks. Battling for its share of the light and water, its single root delved deeper and deeper into the rich hillside loam to take what moisture it could find.

For the first few years the sycamore seemed to be losing the battle. The trees around it had been planted as two year old saplings and were beginning to shoot away, spreading their young branches leaving the sycamore behind. They threatened to starve it of light and water. A continuous struggle that the young sycamore seemed destined to lose. Although for the next four years it held on, each year more difficult than the previous one, each year likely to be it's last.

But then luck played a part, if a tree can be lucky. The plantation was six years old, when one late spring evening the woodman came. What he wanted the timber for who knows? He only took twelve of the straightest and strongest saplings, chopping them off at ground level with a couple of blows from his axe. He didn't even give our sycamore a second look, passing it by for the older trees around it. He wandered around for another twenty minutes, before he took away another couple of young trees. An Ash and an Oak from right next to our tree. This was the chance the sycamore needed and it freed up the necessary light and space for the sycamore to grow, and flourish in the coming years. And it did flourish, for the next one hundred and fifteen years, growing bigger and stronger with each passing summer. From its lofty vantage point on the edge of the woods it stood and watched, and saw many changes to the surrounding landscape. The town grew bigger and bigger, the march of buildings threatening to blot out the view of the church spire. A new dual carriageway now ran along the bottom of the valley, where once deer had come down to drink at the fast flowing stream. The road brought with it the constant hum of traffic which drowned out the song of the sky lark. The badgers too could now not be heard, they had been gone for about forty years now. Gassed by an over zealous farmer during the TB scare of the sixties. Ten years later it was the turn of the Elms to disappear, they

had grown up with the sycamore, but were now to vanish forever. There were still the rabbits, although they had only just clung on when man had decided to cull them with a new disease he had invented, and even now it occasionally resurfaced to take its toll on the population. Through two world wars the Sycamore had stood and watched. Watched as young men left never to return and watched as the skies filled with aircraft heading towards the cities to discharge their deadly loads. It had stood as storms ravaged the countryside and blew trees down around it. Watched as acorns buried by jays began to sprout through and race to replace the casualties. The sycamore had made many friends, the birds that nested in its numerous branches, the cattle and deer that sought shade beneath its huge green canopy. The flowers that had thrived on the wooded slopes and of course the children who climbed among and swung from its branches. The lovers who sought a refuge from prying eyes, those same lovers returning a few years later with their children and then eventually an old lady returning alone. She remembered as did the Sycamore her husband, her children now all gone. Whatever else had happened in her life, the Sycamore had remained constant. It had been there at the beginning and with her all the way through, the sycamore had seen it all and flourished, but now it was nearly over.

A big white sign told of its future.

A DEVELOPMENT OF FIVE BEDROOMED LUXURY HOMES

The Loneliest Conker Tree in the Whole World

The brightest most beautiful emerald green ever seen

The loneliest conker tree in the entire whole world. There it stands all alone at the edge of a barren and empty ploughed field. Majestic in all its guises, but perhaps now in winter time, just a little sinister. No sad or perhaps melancholy may be a better word. Dark and windswept against the grey January sky. At the mercy of the storms that sweep across this bare hedge less landscape. Rain lashed and cold, it stands sentinel like rising up from the ground with not even a blackbird for company. It was waiting, waiting for a sign, just as it had always waited. What exactly that sign was, I'm not sure. Maybe the distant calling of geese bidding farewell to their winter feeding grounds, or the first green shoots pushing through the brown earth below. It could just be a sun filled day, or the song of a thrush. Whatever it is, the tree just needs that little bit of encouragement to start another year. The soil will begin to warm and with it the sap will begin to rise. Slowly at first, forcing its way up. Working its way through the trunk, quickening as it reaches the first branches. Pushing up higher into the outermost twigs, coursing through the trees veins and into its sticky brown buds. Themselves holding onto their secret until they can hold on no more. They succumb to the pressure and explode open, with an almost audible display of colour. The brightest most beautiful emerald green ever seen.

Before the month has passed the leaves are joined by huge white candle like flowers. From dark foreboding to a grand majesty, in just a few short weeks. With the colour comes life, insects first taking their fill from the sweet nectar filled flowers. Quickly followed by hungry birds, some recently arrived from distant shores, and eager to renew their friendship with an old acquaintance and guardian.

Summer time, a time for growing, a time for the green canopy to stretch out and offer shade to a weary farmer or occasional walker. The white flowers now gone and replaced by small green fruits that quickly begin to swell, their sheer abundance promising a bumper harvest. Then with the lengthening days and the rising temperatures moisture is at a premium, some of the fruits not yet ripe begin to fall. Not all of them just enough to make those remaining upon the tree the most perfect seed. The chosen few continue to grow and swell and assume an almost alien like appearance. Spiky and uninviting they jealously guard their hidden fruit.

Now we are there, and as the days begin to grow shorter, the leaves begin to look a little tired and worn. The prickly green orbs fall to the ground, bursting open to reveal their bounty. A shining jewel fit to adorn any crown. A most striking sheen brighter than the most highly polished state dining table. A magnificent sight to behold.

The conker, wrapped away through the growing season. It's as big a miracle as a butterfly appearing from its cocoon, or a frog from a tadpole. The cygnet growing up to be a swan, it's got nothing on a conker. The tree has invested a lot into this seed and given the chance it will repay this investment.

Only for this tree the investment will not be repaid. The months of nurturing and growing were all for nothing. Now as it bids goodbye to its summer companions it also bids goodbye to its future. Yes its seeds litter the fertile soil below, but the farmer begins to plough, spray and sow his own bounty. This is no place for young trees. Not one will be given a chance to produce its own seeds and flowers, to spend its summers with birds and bees. There will be no chance to grow and usher in the spring or kiss summer goodbye. That's why this year I'm going to help. The old chestnuts looking a bit tired now, leaning a little one way. Those winter storms and northerly winds have taken their toll. Who knows how much longer it will last? How many more winter gales or summer droughts it will see? It would be a shame if not one of those jewels was given a chance. That's why this year, I'm going to help.

Dusk

I will bid you goodbye
nay goodnight

Dusk that bit in between night and day. When the world gets ready for bed and hands over to the night shift, but dusk! The word hardly does it justice. It's not as simple as just turning off a light, or as the difference between night and day. Its not just daylight to darkness, there is more to it than that, and we call it dusk. We draw the curtains, settle down for the night and that's it, dusk over and done with. Well it shouldn't be, because it's not as simple as that.

You see it can last for hours and be as different as each passing day. It can come with the speed of an impending storm or flicker out gently with a beautiful soft glow. It can be magnificent and fiery or dark and grey. The light of day does not usually give way easily to the blackness of night. It's not like turning off your reading lamp and closing your eyes. It is a slow process that reveals the world in different shades, each day departing with its own special farewell.

A January day may leave us with drifts of snow and an artificial light to accompany us through the long hours of quiet that always seem to go hand in hand with a heavy snowfall. Then there is April, stormy, windy April, the topmost boughs of the trees clattering together, high in the ever darkening sky. While down below warblers begin to doubt the wisdom of their early arrival, as the warmth of the day is replaced, by a cold almost winters night. Down on the woodland floor the first clammering of spring can be heard, but they to will have too wait until the morning.

Autumn evenings well they seem to wave goodbye, as the gold's and reds mirror the sunset and leave us awestruck at nature's grandeur. All have pleasures but I do have a favourite. Early June, glorious June, flaming June, not quite sure whether it's summer yet or not. Everywhere seems to be still in the throes of spring, the greens remain fresh and bright, and the birds busy with their offspring. Everywhere is life and no amount of light will sate the appetite for life that has taken over the countryside. Dusk in June is a long drawn out affair, as the sun begins its slow descent from the sky. The bright blue begins to fade and with the change of colour comes the first calls to roost. The blackbird just beginning to say his goodnight that will continue for another couple of hours. The wood pigeons leave the fields, they too are heading home. Rooks and Crows also join the exodus, their harsh rasping calls signalling an end to the days feeding. The shadows cast on the still warm grass grow longer as that inky blue time edges still closer. The first star shows in the not yet dark sky and look down on the still feeding swifts, not yet ready to succumb. As if in preparation for the hours ahead, and a warning to all the creatures of the day, a Tawny owl begins its incessant screeching. Beneath the ground the first signs of movement begin, as badgers wake from their days slumber. Finally, as the circle of fire edges ever lower and eventually disappears beneath a distant horizon, a silence descends upon the world, as if mourning the passing of another day.

Goodnight.

Go on, have a look outside......